TODO ACERCA DEL OTOÑO/ALL ABOUT FALL

La cosecha de manzanas/
Apple Harvest

por/by Calvin Harris

Traducción/Translation: Dr. Martín Luis Guzmán Ferrer
Editor consultor/Consulting Editor: Dra. Gail Saunders-Smith

Capstone
press

Mankato, Minnesota

Pebble Plus is published by Capstone Press,
151 Good Counsel Drive, P.O. Box 669, Mankato, Minnesota 56002.
www.capstonepress.com

1 2 3 4 5 6 14 13 12 11 10 09

Library of Congress Cataloging-in-Publication Data
Harris, Calvin.
    [Apple harvest. Spanish & English]
    La cosecha de manzanas = Apple harvest / por/by Calvin Harris.
    p. cm. — (Pebble plus/Todo acerca del otoño/All about fall)
    Includes index.
    Summary: "Simple text and photographs present an apple harvest in fall — in both English and
Spanish" — Provided by publisher.
    ISBN-13: 978-1-4296-3259-1 (hardcover)
    ISBN-10: 1-4296-3259-3 (hardcover)
    1. Apples — Harvesting — Juvenile literature. I. Title. II. Title: Apple harvest. III. Series.
SB363.H2918 2009
634'.11 — dc22   2008034505

Editorial Credits
Sarah L. Schuette, editor; Katy Kudela, bilingual editor; Adalín Torres-Zayas, Spanish copy editor;
    Veronica Bianchini, designer; Charlene Deyle, photo researcher

Photo Credits
Capstone Press/Karon Dubke, 1, 5, 7, 9, 11, 13, 15, 17, 19
Corbis/James Marshall, 21
Shutterstock/MBWTE Photos, cover

Pebble Plus thanks Emma Krumbees in Belle Plaine, Minnesota and Sponsel's Minnesota Harvest in Jordan,
    Minnesota, for the use of their locations during photo shoots.

Note to Parents and Teachers

The Todo acerca del otoño/All about Fall set supports national science standards related
to changes during the seasons. This book describes and illustrates the fall apple harvest
in both English and Spanish. The images support early readers in understanding the text.
The repetition of words and phrases helps early readers learn new words. This book also
introduces early readers to subject-specific vocabulary words, which are defined in the
Glossary section. Early readers may need assistance to read some words and to use the
Table of Contents, Glossary, Internet Sites, and Index sections of the book.

Table of Contents

Tabla de contenidos

Fall Is Here

It's fall. Cool breezes
blow through the
apple orchard trees.

Llegó el otoño

Es otoño. Una brisa fresca
sopla en la huerta
de manzanas.

4

Red apples hang down
from the woody branches.

Rojas manzanas cuelgan de
las ramas de madera rugosa.

The ripe apples are
ready to be picked.
Fall is harvest time.

Las manzanas maduras están
listas para que las recojan.
El otoño es tiempo de cosecha.

Picking Apples

Farmers pick the

apples by hand.

Vamos a recoger manzanas

El campesino recoge

las manzanas a mano.

Workers sort the apples by flavor. The apples are put into bags for shoppers to buy.

Los trabajadores ordenan las manzanas por sabores. Las manzanas se ponen en bolsas para que los clientes las compren.

12

Fun with Apples

Apples make fun treats. Crisp caramel apples are sticky and sweet.

A divertirse con las manzanas

Las manzanas pueden ser divertidos antojitos. Las manzanas recubiertas de caramelo crujiente son pegajosas y dulces.

15

Hot apple cider
warms you up
on a cold day.

El jugo de manzana
caliente puede calentarte
en un día frío.

Apple slices fill the
inside of apple pies.

Las rebanadas de manzana
rellenan el interior del
pastel de manzana.

Other Signs of Fall

The apple harvest has begun.
What are other signs
that it's fall?

Otras señales del otoño

La cosecha de manzanas
empezó. ¿Qué otras señales
hay que es otoño?

20

Glossary

breeze — a gentle wind

cider — a drink made by pressing the juice out of apples

flavor — how something tastes

harvest — to gather or pick crops that are ripe

orchard — a field or farm where fruit trees grow; some apple orchards have hundreds of trees.

ripe — ready to be picked or eaten

slice — a thin, flat piece cut from something larger

sort — to put into groups; apples are often sorted by color and flavor.

Glosario

la brisa — viento suave

cosechar — recoger o juntar cultivos que están maduros

la huerta — campo o granja donde crecen árboles frutales; algunas huertas tienen cientos de árboles.

el jugo de manzana — bebida que se hace sacando el zumo de la manzana

maduro — listo para recogerse o comerse

ordenar — poner en grupos; las manzanas a menudo se ordenan por colores y sabores.

la rebanada — pieza delgada y plana que se corta de algo más grande

el sabor — a lo que sabe una cosa

23

Internet Sites

FactHound offers a safe, fun way to find educator-approved Internet sites related to this book.

Here's what you do:

1. Visit *www.facthound.com*
2. Choose your grade level.
3. Begin your search.

This book's ID number is 9781429632591.

FactHound will fetch the best sites for you!

Index

Sitios de Internet

FactHound te brinda una forma segura y divertida de encontrar sitios de Internet relacionados con este libro y aprobados por docentes.

Lo haces así:

1. Visita *www.facthound.com*
2. Selecciona tu grado escolar.
3. Comienza tu búsqueda.

El número de identificación de este libro es 9781429632591.

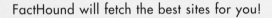

¡FactHound buscará los mejores sitios para ti!

Índice